These STORIES were written by:

_____

NAME

_____

AGE

ABOUT ME
the author

The people and animals I live with are: _____

_____

_____

_____

_____

_____

_____

Some things I love to do are: _____

_____

_____

_____

_____

_____

_____

_____

Something I can't wait to try is: _____

_____

_____

_____

_____

_____

_____

_____

_____

_____

In the *future*, I'd like to write a story about: _____

_____

_____

_____

_____

_____

_____

_____

_____

_____

Words are a writer's tools. There are so many to choose from!
And it's exciting to try out a new word and see what you can do with it.

The words in this list are called *adjectives*, which means they are words
that describe something. How many of the words below have you used before?
Which ones will you use in your next story? If there's a word you don't know,
ask an adult what it means or look it up in a dictionary!

Amazing	Howling	Secretive
Bouncy	Invisible	Shiny
Bristly	Itchy	Silver
Chilly	Jiggly	Soft
Crunchy	Jumpy	Sour
Dark	Knotted	Speckled
Dry	Lonely	Summery
Exciting	Marvelous	Surprising
Flat	Messy	Tremendous
Fragile	Mysterious	Tired
Fuzzy	Noisy	Valuable
Gentle	Open	Warm
Golden	Peaceful	Windy
Grassy	Prickly	Wooly
Hard	Quiet	Wrinkled
Hopeful	Rough	Zippy